Contents

All the words that appear in **bold** are explained in the Glossary on page 30.

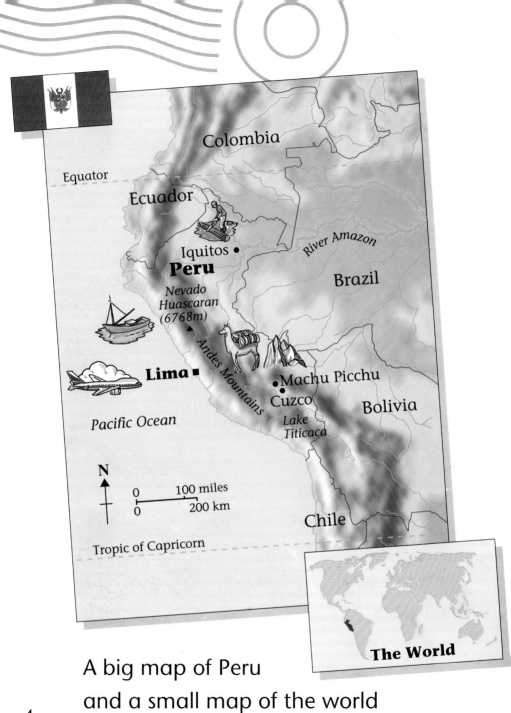

A big map of Peru
and a small map of the world

Dear Amy,

We are in South America.
This country is called Peru.
The plane took more than 15
hours to fly here from London.
You can see Peru marked in red
on the small map.

Love,

Arran

P.S. Mum says that Peru is about five times
bigger than Britain. More than 22 million
people live in Peru. Most people live beside the
sea. Some people live in the mountains.

The busy main square in Lima

Dear Nelson,

Lima is the **capital** city of Peru. About 500 years ago, people from Spain came to Peru. They ruled Peru for more than 200 years. That is why many buildings in Lima look Spanish.

Love,

Pam

P.S. Most people in Peru speak and write in Spanish. Luckily for us, Mum can speak Spanish. She understands what people are saying.

Buying food at the market

Dear Paula,

People in Peru shop for food at the open air markets. I bought a snack from a street stall. It was called *papa rellena*. It was a potato stuffed with vegetables and then fried.

Love,

Ella

P.S. Mum says that one of the first peoples to live in Peru were called the Incas. People in Peru enjoy food that is cooked in the **traditional** Inca way.

A ferry boat on Lake Titicaca

Dear Jed,

This is the biggest lake in South America. It is called Lake Titicaca. It is high up in the mountains. The weather is cooler here. Many people live beside the lake.

Your friend,

William

P.S. We went for a ride across the lake on a **ferry** boat. It was full of people. From the boat, we saw a fisherman. He was in a boat which was made from **reeds** called *tortora*.

A railway station in the Andes mountains

Dear Clare,

Yesterday we rode on a train. It carried us across the Andes Mountains. The train was full of **tourists**. At the top of the mountains, Dad took some photos. The view was fantastic.

Love,

Liam

P.S. Dad says that most people in Peru travel by bus. In the high mountains, people ride on animals called llamas. Some places are so remote that you have to get there by plane.

Shopping in the mountains

Dear Hugo,

There are many villages high in the mountains. In one village we bought some woollen rugs. We paid for them with Peruvian money called *nuevo sol*.

See you soon,

James

P.S. Mum says that 700 years ago the Inca peoples ruled Peru. They ruled for about 200 years. The Incas were good farmers, builders and craft workers.

The ruins of Machu Picchu

Dear Petra,

We have reached the ruins of Machu Picchu. There are lots of tourists here. The Inca peoples built this ancient city. Nobody has lived in Machu Picchu for hundreds of years.

Your friend,

Rachel

P.S. Dad says that when the Spanish people came to Peru, they did not find Machu Picchu. The city stayed hidden for about 400 years. An explorer discovered it in 1911.

Houses on the River Amazon at Iquitos

Dear Jordan,

We are in the city of Iquitos. These floating houses are on the edge of the city. People travel by boat along the River Amazon to visit other towns and villages.

Love,

Elroy

P.S. The plane flew over mountains and **rainforests** to reach Iquitos. Iquitos is on an island in the River Amazon. It is very hot here in the **tropics**.

In the Amazon rainforest

Dear Ali,

The Amazon rainforest is full of plants, wild animals and birds. In the forest, **native** peoples live by hunting for food. The people have lived this way for thousands of years.

Love,

Githa

P.S. Mum says that the River Amazon rises in the Andes Mountains. It is the longest river in the world. Big ships can sail for about 3,000 miles along this river.

A fishing boat made from reeds

Dear Abigail,

Here we are beside the Pacific Ocean. The fishermen here use long, narrow, *tortora* reed boats. People in Peru have used boats like these for hundreds of years.

Love,

Rose

P.S. We are staying in a smart new house near the beach. Mum says that not long ago, this place was a quiet fishing village. Now it is full of people on holiday.

Playing music on the street

Dear Jack,

I love the music in Peru. Everywhere you go there are *Mestizo* bands. Long ago, the Incas played music on the same kinds of instruments.

Love,

Megan

P.S. People in Peru like to enjoy themselves. They love football, basketball and baseball. Today there was a **bullfight**. Many people think that bullfighting is cruel.

A big procession at a festival

Dear Sara,

Most people in Peru follow the **Christian** religion. People dress up for **festivals**. This one is called *Corpus Christi*. People walk through the streets together in a procession.

Love,

Tom

P.S. Dad says that there are many festivals in Peru. Some are part of the Christian religion. Others are to remember events from the time of the Inca peoples.

The flag of Peru at the
Government Palace, Lima

Dear Anna,

This has been the flag of Peru for more than 100 years. It has two red stripes and one white stripe. In the middle of the white stripe there is a badge which stands for Peru.

Your friend,

Josh

P.S. Mum says that Peru is no longer ruled by Spain. The people of Peru choose their own leaders. This way of ruling is called a **democracy**.

Glossary

Bullfight: A fight between men and a bull.

Capital: The town or city where people who rule the country meet.

Christians: People who follow the teachings of Jesus. Jesus lived about 2,000 years ago.

Democracy: A country where all the people choose the leaders they want to run the country.

Ferry: A large boat which carries people across water.

Festival: A time when people remember something or someone special from the past. People often sing and dance during a festival.

Native: Someone who was born in the place or part of the country where they live.

P.S.: This stands for Post Script. A postscript is the part of a card or letter which is added at the end, after the person has signed it.

Rainforest: Forests near the middle of the Earth. The weather there is hot and wet.

Reeds: Plants which grow beside rivers or lakes. They have long, thin leaves which are very strong.

Tourist: A person who is on holiday away from home.

Traditional: Something which has been done in the same way for a long time in the past.

Tropics: The lands which are near the middle of the Earth. The heat from the sun is strongest here. We draw lines on maps to show the position of the tropics.

Index